Discover Simple, Super Effective Ways to Make Your Child a Reader

PRAISE of the Book

"This is an audacious and powerful read! This suggests us great parenting style which can mould children for great nation."

— Dr. VK Goswami
Visiting Scientist; UNIDO, ICTP, ITALY, Expert Panel, NOAA, UNV, ICAO & AIU Rosters Vice Chancellor

"If you know anyone caring for someone facing certain problems regarding their children, this book could be the best gift ever."

— Dr. Ridwana Sanam
Founder & Managing Director (KRV Group) and Author of "How to Write off Your Pain"

"A book of great inspiration, courage, and hope, every word rings with truth, kindness, and the beauty of the human spirit."

— Green Man Vijaypal Baghel
Renowned Environmentalist/Honored as Social Reformers of India by Wikipedia

This book is selected by National Book Trust(NBT), Government of India at:

- ▶ **Cape Town Book Fair (South Africa), 2012**
- ▶ **Sharjah International Book Fair (UAE), 2013**

DISCOVER SIMPLE, SUPER EFFECTIVE WAYS TO MAKE YOUR CHILD A READER

Learn how to make your child super-active in Reading

Worldwide Published by
Pendown Press

PENDOWN PRESS

An ISO 9001 & ISO 14001 Certified Co.,

Regd. Office: 2525/193, 1st Floor, Onkar Nagar-A,
Tri Nagar, Delhi-110035

Ph.: 09350849407, 09312235086

E-mail: info@pendownpress.com

Branch Office: 1A/2A, 20, Hari Sadan, Ansari Road,
Daryaganj, New Delhi-110002

Ph.: 011-45794768

Website: PendownPress.com

Revised Edition: 2019
Price: ₹279/-
ISBN: 978-93-81970-05-8

Layout and Cover Designed by Pendown Graphics Team
Printed and Bound in India by Thomson Press India Ltd.

Contents

Few Words

We all want to do the best we can to help our children, and developing effective literacy is probably the most important skill they will ever learn.

Determine what kind of reader your child is. Some children don't like reading and have a tendency to avoid it at all costs – these children usually take the most work to help. Other children don't mind reading, but usually only read in order to satisfy requirements for school. Then, there are the children who not only read for school, but also for fun. It is important to recognize the kind of reader your child is. After you figure out what type of reader your child is, determine if your child needs any kind of physical aid, such as glasses. The vocabulary of your child is integral to his or her reading capabilities. Help your child increase his or her vocabulary by creating word lists from texts. Read these texts with your child and discuss the new words. Guide your child in figuring out what words mean by the context in which they're used. Then, use the new words around the house.

It's important to determine what areas your child needs help in as a reader. You can talk with your child's teacher, counselor or any other learning professional working with your child to determine what needs to be done. Whether your child is advanced for his or her age or struggling, it's still important to continually practice reading skills.

Introduce your child to the world of reading as early as possible. Familiarize him with books. Encourage reading at home on a daily basis. Set aside a time each night for family reading. There are many children's literature book lists available online and at libraries. Go over the list with your child and allow him or her to pick out a number of books. The more your child reads for personal pleasure, the more his or her reading skills are likely to improve.

- GPH Panel of Experts

Acknowledgements

The GPH Panel of Experts wishes to acknowledge the extensive efforts of staff members in gathering the information for and editing this book. The Panel also extends a special thanks to the following people who reviewed and provided feedback on the content of this work:

Dinesh Verma

CEO, GullyBaba Publishing House Pvt. Ltd.

Mahesh Chand

– Editor

Anita Verma

— Critique

Syed Makhdoom Ali

— Editor

1 INTRODUCTION

"What can you do to promote world peace?
Go home and love your family."
~ *Mother Teresa*

There is a widespread belief that a child starts responding to its surroundings the day he is born. But, contrary to the popular belief, the child starts responding to the sounds outside his mother's womb as his mother progresses from 27th week of her pregnancy. Reading a book to your baby can be beneficial for your baby-to-born as early as this stage. A good book read at this stage, apart from helping him stimulate emotions, does also help to prepare him for the life after his birth.

Therefore, if you are among those parents who think that your baby is too young to Reap the Rewards of reading, think again. The recent researches have left us with little doubt that it is never too early to start enjoying books with your new born.

To understand the connection between a child's early experiences with spoken language and learning to read, you might think of language as a four-legged stool.

LSRW
LISTENING-SPEAKING-READING-WRITING

They are the four skills of a language, and are inter-related. One needs to understand and enhance on these skills in coordination, so as to enable smooth ACQUISITION of language.

This book will prove to be extremely instrumental to help you understand as to how you can help your child become a leader and make him unlock the mysteries of the world and have an access to the treasure of knowledge at a very young age. After reading this book, you will be able to:

- Talk with and listen to your child.
- Read together with him.
- Help your child to learn about books and print.
- Encourage your child's early writing efforts.
- Help your child to learn English if it is not his first language.

Children are made readers on the lap of their parents

- Make your child an effective reader through Simple and Super Effective ways

It is said that teaching through activity is the most effective way. This book contains several easy-to-understand, easier-to-perform activities that will help your child's learning as entertaining as his most favourite play.

However, these activities are only a starting point. We hope that you and your child will enjoy them enough to create and try many more on your own. As a parent, you are your child's first teacher. You don't need to be the best reader to help — your time and interest and the pleasure that you share with your child as part of reading together are what really count. A few names of some books and websites are also given to help you take this forward.

Here, it is important to know that reading is sensitive to age group for each age-group has different cognitive skills and different levels of skills.

We all know that older children can do so many things that younger ones can't. This is true for reading, too. In order to understand certain learning steps of children, this book ties the discussion and activities to four age groups:

- Baby = birth to 1 year
- Toddler = 1 to 3 years
- Pre-schooler = ages 3 and 4
- Kindergartner/early first-grader = ages 5 and 6

> You can read to a newborn also. Your baby will get connected to the sound of your voice and relate to.

Keep in mind, however, that all children don't learn at the same pace. And even though they learn new things, they may have "old favorites" — books and activities from early years that they still enjoy. Ultimately, you are the best person to decide which activities will work best for your child.

Your child becomes capable of handling books since the time he is able to sit.

Children do not become readers by the time their parents want them to be. It is important thing to take into consideration. If the elder sibling/first cousin/second cousin of a child was able to read in the age he is in, but he is still struggling a bit, that does not mean, he needs special care, special training, reprimand, etc. They become readers step by step—by learning bit a bit, one thing after the other. By age 7, most children are reading. When children receive the right kind of help in their early years, reading difficulties that can arise later in their lives can be prevented. This book offers steps that you can take to make your child move on the way to becoming a successful reader. It is an adventure that you will not want to miss, and the benefits for your child will last lifetime.

Let your child enjoy the touch and feel of a book. Select books with brightly-coloured pictures.

xxx

2 BECOMING A READER

"If you are a parent, open doors to unknown directions to the child so he can explore. Don't make him afraid of the unknown, give his support."
~ *Osho*

Every step a child takes towards learning to read leads to betterment, and is a link to the other. Bit by bit, the child builds the knowledge that is necessary for being a reader. Over their first 6 years, most children:

- Talk and listen.
- Listen to stories read aloud.
- Pretend to read.
- Learn how to handle books.
- Learn about print and how it works.
- Identify letters by name and shape.

- Identify separate sounds in spoken language.
- Write with scribbles and drawing.
- Connect single letters with the sounds they make.
- Connect what they already know to what they read.
- Predict what will come next in stories and poems.
- Connect combinations of letters with sounds.
- Recognize simple words in print.
- Sum up what a story is about.
- Write individual letters of the alphabet.
- Write words.
- Write simple sentences.
- Read simple books.
- Write to communicate.

Children can take more than one of these steps at the same time. This list of steps, though gives you a general idea of how your child will progress towards becoming a better reader.

Learn about the Learning Style of your Child

Each and every child has his exclusive learning preferences and styles. By and large, no any child is bad in learning. If we impose one way of learning on the child who does not identify himself with that way, we make a mistake of calling him a bad learner.

There are seven fundamental learning steps: Verbal, Auditory, Visual, Physical, Logical(mathematical), Social and Solitary. For example, children who are auditory learners, lest best by hearing to things explained. Similarly, children who are visual learners, learn things best by seeing a video, visual effects, or presentation, etc. Therefore, before making your child to learn, it is imperative for you to know about his learning style.

From the very beginning, babies try to imitate the sounds that they hear from us. They "read" the looks on our faces and movements. That's why it is so important to talk, sing, smile, and make gesture to your child.

Hearing you talk is your baby's very first step towards becoming a reader, because it helps him to love language and learn words.

As your child progresses in age increase the intensity of interaction with him.

Take a keen interest in the things he does. Ask him to tell what he did the entire day—the stuff he read, the topic on which he read, the teacher/s he interacted with, the friends he talked to, the gift(if any) that he got, the thing he liked the most and why and listen to what he says to you with rapt attention. Ignore, if a person calls to you in between. If you want to correct/ make addition to it, first appreciate what he says and then with smile on your face, you may start like: Ohho.. great.. that means you are learning at a great pace. Engage your child in talking and listening. With these, you are also encouraging your child to think as he speaks. In addition, you are also showing that you respect his knowledge and his ability to keep learning.

Reading Together

Imagine sitting your baby in your lap and reading a book to him for the first time.

> Hold your baby in your lap when you read to him. You may also put him on chair or a particular spot, if he is comfortable.

How different from just talking! Now you're showing him pictures. Mind, one picture is like 1000 words. This is one of the best ways to familiarize your child with the world of books.

You point out to them. In a lively way, you explain what the pictures are. You've just helped your child to take the next step beyond talking. You've shown him that words and pictures connect. And you've activated his way to understanding and enjoying books.

While your child is still a baby, reading aloud to him should become part of your daily routine. Mind, your child is never too young for books. Reading aloud to your baby of just six months of age will help him build a strong vocabulary and better early literacy skills four years later, when he will start going to school. This is the finding of the Pediatric Academic Societies' Meeting held at May 8, 2017.

According to developmental psychologist Carolyn Cates, a research assistant professor in the department of pediatrics at NYU Langone Medical Center,

"Even though children may not be thinking yet, that does not mean they are not learning."

Pick a quiet time, such as just before you put him to bed. This will give him a chance to rest between play and sleep. If you can, read with him in your lap or snuggled next to you so that he feels close and safe. As he progresses in age, he may need to move around, as you read to him. If he gets tired or restless, stop reading. Take this as a cue, that he is losing interest. Make reading aloud a quiet and comfortable activity so that your child looks forward to. Chances are very good that he will like reading all the more because of it.

Your child will love books with pictures of children.

Try to spend at least 30 minutes each day reading to and with your child. Initially, read for no more than a few minutes at a time, several times a day. As your child progresses in age, you should be able to tell if he wants you to read for longer periods. Don't be discouraged if you have to skip a day or don't always keep to your schedule. Just get back to your daily routine as soon as you can. Make sure that reading remains fun for both of you!

Reading books with children is one of the most important things that parents can do to help their children become readers.

What does It Mean?

From the earliest days, talk with your child about what you are reading. You might point to pictures and name what is in them. When he is ready, have him do the same.

For example, ask your child to show you the picture of a doll/dog/parrot which is in the book. If he is able to find, give him a gentle pat on his chin or back in appreciation. Read his mood; if he is enjoying, tell him to find the other picture and increase the time of this activity. The longer you are able to make your child engaged in spotting you the asked picture, the more he will learn about the things that surround him.

As the boy progresses in age and becomes able to take interest in small stories, select a book that might be a fun and right for your child. Read the book slowly, and take a pause very often in the beginning, preferably after every paragraph. Use the pause time to explain the paragraph to your child. If he does not show much interest in the very first 2-3 paragraphs, do not burden your child by continuing the story. Choose another story, you are more sure, your child will pick interest in.

By the time your child is able to talk, ask him some questions about the story like, “What do you think will happen next?” or “Do you know what this palace is?” Answer him questions and, if you think he doesn’t understand something, stop and talk more about what he asked. Don’t worry if you occasionally break the flow of a story to make clear something that is important. However, don’t stop so often to the point that the child loses track of what is happening in the story.

Make bookstore visit your habit so that your child grows up with that habit.

Choosing the Correct Books!!

The books that you pick to read with your child are very important. If you aren’t sure of what books are right for your child, ask a librarian or a friend with knowledge of books to help you choose titles.

Choose books carefully. Remember, your child may not necessarily enjoy reading the book/s you did when you were his age. Do not force your favourite on him.

Introduce your child to books when he is a baby. Let him hold and play with books made just for babies.

Books in any one of the following categories will help your child make a smart start:

1. Nursery Rhymes and Poetry: Rhyming verses happen to be very close to a baby—just like a heartbeat. You can find the illustrated versions of classical rhymes and lullabies for your darling dear. Given the short attention span of your child, poems and nursery rhymes could be a good match, since he can read one in a minute or two. And do not expect your child to

- Read every page
- Read the pages in sequence
- Read word to word

Just let your child hold and manipulate the book.

2. Concept Books: The high-contrast images will be the easiest for your child to see, as the vision of your child is still developing. If your child is under 18 months of age, the book with one clear photograph, or graphic drawing per page will be the best buy. These books will help your child get introduced with letters, shapes, colours, animals and more.

Child psychologists have proved beyond reasonable doubts that babies love seeing other tiny tots. Therefore, you should buy the books that use baby faces to show emotions or chores(playing, bathing, eating, etc.).

3. Board Books: There are plenty of concept books (along with classic tales and storybooks) available in the market. These types of books will activate the thought process of your baby and make him experiment: What is this? Can I hold it? Ohho no.. This one is ok to hold. I have held it now. Should I taste it? And all these explorations help the baby quickly and in a playful mood.

4. Wordless Books: A book, becomes boring as it contains words. A word-less book does not have any such risks. Moreover, the wordless version of a book, is very effective in promoting freewheeling chats with your child about the book.

5. Question-and-answer Books: Stories that contain a question or follow a pattern strengthen your baby's language skills. After knowing about the pattern of the book, he will soon get prompted to think analytically to answer that may come at the end of a story, he is learning.

6. Interactive Books: Even your infant will love these types of books. As he learns from his senses, it makes good senses to add touching to the learning and seeing aspects of reading.

Choose books with covers that have big, colourful pictures of things that he sees every day. Don't be upset if at first your child chews or throws a book. Be patient. Cuddling with the child as you point to and talk with great excitement about the book's pictures will soon capture his interest. When your baby becomes a toddler, he will enjoy choosing books to read.

POP OUT books and colourful books with images and pictures are generally popular with the kids. These types of books make them interesting and inclined towards reading.

As your child grows into a pre-schooler there are some proven ways following which you can make him a reader for sure. Given below are these ways:

1. Let your child "pretend to read": It will be really great if he picks up a book and imitates the act of reading. Even if he is not able to decode the words on the pages, it is important that he gets exposed early to the physical tasks of reading.

2. Read together every day: Make this a special event to the extent that your child starts looking forward to every day. Make a comfortable reading nook in your house, or sit together in a specious chair. Now, start reading a story. While selecting a story, make sure that your child takes keen interest. Get involved with him, leaving behind all your other important engagements. Do not even attend a mobile call, if it is not very urgent. This will help create a positive association with reading.

3. Talk about your Love of Reading: Let your child know as to how much you enjoy reading together.

If you have any, share your favourite childhood books and talk about why it is special for you. Tell him how you become able to learn good things in your life with the help of this book, underlining the importance of reading.

4. Know when to Stop: If your child loses interest or is struggling to pay attention to read the book, put the book away for a while. You do not have to make him feel that reading is something that becomes boring after a while.

5. Be Interactive: Do not let him alone when he is reading. Be with him like his shadow, point out and explain the words, paragraph, page, etc. Illustrate the story and tell him as to what the character's expressions suggest. Do not ignore your child's query/doubt.

Keep in mind that young children most often enjoy books about people, places, and things that are like those they know. But mystery, fairy tales and visuals fascinate them the most. They are happy to see the pictures of bodies, huge flowers, nature, animals, celestial bodies, animated pictures. The books can be about where you live or your culture, your holidays, or the way you dress. If your child has special interests, such as dinosaurs or basket ball, look for books about those interests.

From your child's toddler years to early first grade, you should also look for books of poems and rhymes. Remember when your baby heard your talking sounds and tried to imitate them? Rhymes are an extension of that language skill. As it comes easy to the memory, and it retains the sing-a-song style, they learn well. By hearing and saying rhymes, along with repeated words and phrases, your child learns about spoken sounds and words. Rhymes also spark a child's curiosity about what comes next, which adds fun, and adventure to reading.

You Initiate, Child will Emulate, Follow!!

When you take your child to the library, check out a book for yourself. This sets a good example, as the child sees you reading for yourself. When he sees that you are interested and keen to read, it will encourage him as well. Ask your child to get a book for himself and sit with you as you read your book, magazine/newspaper. It's the reading that counts. When your child sees that reading is important to you, he may decide that it is important to him as well.

> If your child does not like a book you think he might like, read it yourself and make him believe that you are enjoying it to arouse his curiosity.

Learning about Print and Books

Reading together is a perfect time to help a late toddler or early pre-schooler learn what print is. As you read aloud, stop now and then and point to letters and words; then point to the pictures they stand for. Your child will begin to understand that the letters form words and that words name pictures. He will also start to learn that each letter has its own sound — one of the most important things your child can know while learning to read.(Although he will learn phonetics and all this when he grows up).

Nowadays, children start going to a pre-school by 2 years. They are familiar with the alphabet and start with proper reading of small words, by the time they turn 3.

In late kindergarten or early first grade, your child may want to read on his own. Let him! But be sure that he wants to do it. Reading should be something he is proud of and eager to do, and not a lesson! Any activity that the child takes up enthusiastically and on his own, will have a long-term effect on him, and will stay with him for longer, thus becoming a habit.

How does a Book Work?

Children are fascinated by the look and feel of books. They see how easily you handle and read books, and they want to do the same. When your toddler watches you handle books, he begins to learn that a book is for reading, not tearing or tossing around. Before he is 3, he may even pick one up and pretend to read, an important sign that he is beginning to know what a book is for. As your child becomes a pre-schooler, he is learning that:

- A book has a front cover.
- A book has a beginning and an end.
- A book has pages.
- A page in a book has a top and a bottom.
- You turn pages one at a time.
- You read a book from left to right of a page.

As you read with your 4 or five-year-old, begin to remind him about these things. Read the title on the cover. Talk about the picture on the cover. Point to the place where the story starts and, later, where it ends. Let your child help turn the pages. When you start a new page, point to the start of the words and keep following the words by moving your finger beneath them. It takes time for a child to learn these things, but when your child learns them, he solves some of reading mysteries.

Some books of puzzles and rhymes in bold print and big sizes are specifically helpful at this time.

Books are the quietest and most constant of friends; they are the most accessible and wisest of counselors.

When you befriend Book, you make a Friend for Life

Anyone who has befriended the written word, would never be lonely. All booklovers know that they can live several lives, travel innumerable places and do myriad things through their books. You get to see the perspective of another person and find out that you are not the absolute authority on the topic.

Today our living rooms have been invaded by the television and computer. Children spend all the free time glued to either of them.

Books teach a lot to the kids. They expand their vocabularies, helping them later in life. The command of the language increases many fold. It gives a boost to the child's imagination, letting the mind reach the unthinkable and increasing the creativity. Reading about many things vastly improves the child knowledge. For instance you learn more about Africa but reading an interesting story than by the dry course books.

Some parents, in order to introduce their child to the wonderful world of books, make some mistakes. They seem to be emposing interest on them to love books. However, a little commonsense, understanding of the behaviours of the child and the ability to make reading interesting will help the students develop interest in reading books.

Fix a Time for Reading

Keep about half an hour daily reserved for reading time. This can be just before bed time or any other time suitable to both. Initially let them read the books you had recounted as children. The story line will be familiar and it will be easy for them to pick out the words.

Start Young

Interest in books cannot be generated overnight. It is a slow process wherein the child learns to fall in love with the enchanted world of the written world. If the habit of reading is inculcated at the earliest, this will develop slowly as the child grows. Parents have to start as soon as the child is able to understand. Read out stories to your two-year-old child. Slowly replace this story telling to story reading.

Baby Steps

Parents should be realistic in their expectations. Do not think that the child will jump into reading the very first time they get their hands on the book. The first few times they may falter with pronunciations. Gently correct them. They may even read through the whole page without understanding even a single word. Instead of explaining the whole book to them, make their brains work. Ask easy questions about the story. Eventually they will know about deciphering books.

Make your Child Learn by Examples

It is very important to teach the kids by setting an example. Ensure that the children see you read. If you read books your children will automatically do the same. It is very difficult to convince a child to read with concentration if the parents never pick up a book. Not only it will be an inspiration but also the kids will find reading together a lot of fun.

Get Books on Subjects of Interest

If the child is a great Pooh, or is a great fan of a cartoon character, get some books on that character. The markets are abound with a variety of things related to cartoons. Do a little market survey and get the books of the particular character. Ensure that the books are colorful and picturesque. The print should be large as reading small print can be tedious. Go through the books before buying. The words should be of a level understandable by your child. Too easy or too tough books distract the children very easily.

Install Aids

There are many supporting aids the parents can utilize to encourage reading. Set up a bulletin board and put cartoons with funny comments on it. Pin a small limerick or poetry on it for your child to read. You can get an audio book set too. This has a story recorded on tape along with the printed book. The children can catch the nuances of pronunciation as they read along. Put notes in the Tiffin box. Get vocabulary-building games on the computer.

Universal Reading Time

Do not restrict reading to the confines of your room. Utilize the abundance of words floating all around us. Point out the words on the hoardings on the way. Ask the child to read out the credits on the cinema poster. Telling the headlines from the newspaper is a very good way to learn. While you are waiting for the doctor to arrive, they can read up the pamphlets. At the restaurant, let them read the menu and decide on the order. Ask them to decipher the instructions on the new game.

Do not Push

Try all this in a very casual manner. If the child gets feeling that she is being pushed towards reading, she will stall like an adamant horse. It should all seem like a wildly interesting game. For instance, while waiting for the doctor, don't push the pamphlet in the kid's hand and order him to read. Instead, say very, very casually (a bored voice is a must), "There are four words starting with ch in this pamphlet." Immediately the child will try to find out the fact for himself and find a few more words to boot.

These techniques are just general aids to help the children read more. As a parent you have to show enthusiasm towards their new activity. Correct them gently, when wrong. Show enthusiasm and appreciation when the child wants to read. It is a good idea to buy books as gifts and incentive. Discuss the book the child has just read. Talk about his favorite character in the book. If there is a movie made on the particular book, make it a point to take him to it.

Don't force, guide. As soon as the child learns that he HAS to read, it becomes another subject to study, a tiresome chore. Reading should be introduced as a delightful pastime and not a rigorous punishment.

So, go ahead, introduce your kids to the written word and they will never be lonely again.

From Reading to Writing

Early Efforts to Write

Writing and reading should not be viewed in an isolated form. Rather, both these things go hand in hand. In fact, reading is breathing in and writing is breathing out. But, the onus of making him good at both reading and writing, lies on you. If your child reads a particular story and tells you that he really enjoyed reading it, you can prompt him to write about the story—on which subject the story is written, what are the important characters of the story, how the content of the story flows, what are its salient features, what is the summary of the story, so on and so forth.

When he is about 2 years' old, give your child crayons and paper and encourage him to draw and scribble.

He will have fun choosing which colors to use and which shapes to make. As he holds and moves the crayons, he will also develop muscle control. When he is a late toddler or early pre-schooler, he will become as eager to write as he is to read.

Your pre-school child's scribbles or drawings are his first writings. He will soon begin to write the alphabet letters. Writing the letters helps your child learn about their different sounds. His very early learning about letters and sounds gives him ideas about how to spell words. When he begins writing words, don't worry that he doesn't spell them correctly. Instead, praise him for his efforts! In fact, if you look closely, you'll see that he made a pretty good try at spelling a word for the first time. Later on, with help from teachers (and from you); he will learn the right way to spell words. For the moment, however,he has taken a great step towards being a writer!! Applaud him!

Get some picture book for your child. Picture books can convey more through their beautiful illustrations than the books that are rich in content.

Reading In Another Language

In India, English is L2, the second language for everyone. But not being a native speaker of English, will not deter him learn the language and get mastery over it. If you make an environment suitable for learning English, he will definitely pick the language within no time. You can build a separate library for your child and make it stuffed with interesting and inspiring English books. You can choose activities to build the vocabulary of your child and explore his reading and writing skills. You may even start talking to him in English so that he picks up the language of the class easily and do not learn by translating the language in his mother tongue.

When your child first enters school, get familiar with his school and talk his teacher. Teachers welcome such talks. The schools have an orientation program for parents and children both. Regular parent-teacher interactions and meetings are also there.

When you meet, tell the teacher about the things that you are doing/planning to do to help your child become a good learner of English. Ask the teachers about his own methods. If any of his methods merits implementation, implement it in your home as well. Your child will find it easy to do it—both in school and in his home. Mind, both you and the teacher has common goal—to teach your child. You will achieve more, if you work together.

Give them books on topics that interest them, not what you would like them to read!!!

Let Your Child Love to Read

Make It a Treat

Vasud and Khushi have adopted a unique approach to literature. Right from childhood, they've used a story as a reward for good behaviour. So every time Vasud ate his greens or put away his books without being told, he was rewarded with a story. As Vasud grew, his parents bought him books for every little achievement. For Vasud books became a medal. And today, at 12, he is a voracious reader with his own corner in his parents' library.

Set up a Special Area

Mishti is fiercely proud of her little corner in the library. It has her bean bag and own little rack. If space permits, make a small reading area in your children's room, where they can proudly display their literature. It might also make the idea of books more appealing to the gadget-crazy generation that our kids belong to.

Lead by Example

As is true for everything else, teach your kids to read by example. Your kids are always imitating you consciously or subconsciously. If you're glued to TV yourself, your child is hardly going to pay attention to books. But if they see you curled up on the sofa, absorbed in a book, often enough, they're likely to try it themselves. The happiness and satisfaction you get after reading a book is immense; transfer this feeling to your child.

Talk

To TALK is the most effective way of communication. But these conversations can actually be fun. If you and your husband make it a point to discuss books at the dinner table, your children will be tempted to read and contribute to the conversations. But make sure that your kids don't feel left out. If, for example, you're discussing "Immortals of Meluha' or "mahabharata", pepper the conversation with your favourite bits, giving them a gist of the story. Conversely, make sure you read some of your kids' favourites as well. If you make the effort to broaden your horizon, they will too.

Make them Start Young

We know dads who've read to wombs, but you needn't start that young. Start out with baby books with big pictures at an year-plus, teaching words gradually. Soon, the babies will begin to recognize the alphabet. Practice an interactive bedtime story ritual from early on, encouraging your kids to read a little with you...

Adapt

What's important is that your children read, not how they read. If Kindle is the only way to get the classics to them, you'll just have to make your peace with it. Don't restrict your kids to books. Focus on helping your child discover the joy of the written word. Falling in love with books will happen naturally once they develop the habit.

Accept their Interests

Face it, no matter how much you want it, there's a chance your kids might not care a lot about your favorite authors or what you consider 'good reading'. Accept their interests and get them books on subjects of their interests. You might not get superheroes, but if that's all they care about, you need to get them the comics that will keep them glued for hours. It may not be the best source of knowledge and information, but the goal is to get them to start enjoying reading. Once their interests diversify, the subject matter will take care of itself.

xxx

History will judge us by the difference we make in the everyday lives of children.

-Nelson Mandela

3 ACTIVITIES

"Having a baby is a life-changer. It gives you a whole other perspective on why you wake up every day."
~ *Taylor Hanson*

What follows are ideas for language-building activities that you can do with your child to help him to build the skills he needs to become a reader. Most public libraries offer free use of books, magazines, videos, computers, and other services or at minimal charges. Other things that you might need for these activities are not expensive.

For each set of activities, we give an age span that suggests when children should try them. From one activity to the next, we continue to talk about children at different stages: babies (birth to 1 year), toddlers (1 to 3 years), pre-schoolers (ages 3 and 4), and kindergartner/

early first-graders (ages 5 and 6). Remember that children don't always learn the same things at the same pace. And they don't suddenly stop doing one thing and start doing another just because they are a little older. So use the ages as guides as your child learns and grows. Don't consider them to be hard and fast rules. Be flexible with children. Do play games and set out certain rules for activities, as this will also let them be disciplined, yet be flexible.

You'll see that your role in the activities has changed, too. Just as you hold up your child when he learning to walk, you will help him a lot when he's taking his first language step. As he grows, you will gradually let go, and he will take more and more language steps on his own. That is why in most of the activities we say, "The first activities. . . work well with younger children. As your child progresses in age and does, the later activities let him do more."

As a parent, you can help your child learn in a way no one else can. That desire to learn is a key to your child's later success. Enjoyment is important! So, if your child doesn't enjoy one activity, move on to another. You can always return to any activity later on.

Baby Talk

(For babies from birth to 1 year)

Babies love hearing your voice. When you answer your child's sounds with sounds of your own, he learns that what he "says" has meaning and is important to you.

What Can Parents Do?

- Talk to your baby often. Answer his coos, gurgles, and smiles. Talk, touch, and smile back. Get him to look at you.
- Play simple talking and touching games with your baby. Ask, "Where's your nose?" Then touch his nose and say playfully, "There's your nose!" Do this several times, and then switch to an ear or knee or tummy. Stop when he (or you) gets tired of the game.
- Change the game by touching the nose or ear and repeating the word for it several times. Do this with objects too. When he hears you naming something over and over again, your child begins to connect the sound with what it means.
- Do things that interest your baby. Vary your tone of voice, make funny faces, sing lullabies, and recite simple nursery rhymes. Play "peek-a-boo" and "pat- a-cake" with him.

It's so important to talk to your baby! With your help, his/her coos and gurgles will one day give way to words.

Books and Babies

(For babies from age 6 weeks to 1 year)

Sharing books is a way to have fun with your baby and to help him move on the road to becoming a reader.

What Parents Need?

- Cardboard or cloth books with large, simple pictures of things with which babies are familiar
- Lift-the-flap, touch-and-feel, or peep-through play books

What Can Parents Do?

- Read to your baby for short periods several times a day. Bedtime is always a good time, but you can read at other times as well — while you're in the park, on the bus, or even at the breakfast table (without the food!).
- As you read, point out things in the pictures. Name them as you point to them.
- Give your baby sturdy books to look at, touch, and hold. Allow him to peek through the holes or lift the flaps to discover surprises.

Babies soon recognize the faces and voices of those who care for them. As you read to your baby, he will begin to connect books with what he loves most — your voice and closeness.

Chatting with Children

(For children ages 1 to 6)

Continue talking with your older child as you did with your baby. Talking helps him to develop language skills and lets him know that what he says is important.

What Can Parents Do?

The first activities in the list below work well with younger children. As your child progresses in age and begin to take interest in the later activities, let him do more. However, keep doing the first ones as long as he enjoys them.

The first activities given below are best suited for the younger children. As your child progresses in age, advance the activity to let him do/learn more. However, do not snatch any activity from him in the name that he has progressed in age and this activity is no longer meant for him.

- Talk often with your toddler. When feeding, bathing, and dressing him, ask him to name or find different objects or clothing. Point out colors, sizes, and shapes.

- Talk with your child as you read together. Point to pictures and name what is in them. When he is ready, ask him to do the same. Ask him about his favorite parts of the story, and answer his questions about events or characters.
- Teach your toddler to be a helper. Make your toddler a helper by asking him to find things. As you cook, give him pots and pans or measuring spoons to play with. Ask him what he is doing and answer his questions.
- Do not let your Together Time to get wasted. Wherever you go with your child, do not do anything except talking to your child. Make your conversation interactive. Do not use this time to lecture on a particular topic, or why you dislike him for some reasons, what you do not like in one of his friends, why you will not allow him to go a particular place with his uncle, so on and so forth. Instead use it as an opportunity to ask questions that are relevant to his age. For example, "Which flowers are read? What is the name of this market? What do the colours of a traffic light suggest? What profession does this uniform suggest and the likes.

- Listen to your child's questions patiently and answer them patiently as well. If you don't know the answer to a question, have him join you as you look for the answer in a book. He will then see how important books are as sources of information.

If you do not have much idea about books, read our blog on famous books, which changed the lives of many. Just log on to gullybaba.com/blog/books and you will have access to treasure of knowledge regarding books.

- Have your child tell you a story. Then ask him questions, explaining that you need to understand better.

- When he is able, ask him to help you in the kitchen. He might set the table or decorate a batch of cookies. A first-grader may enjoy helping you make a simple recipe. Talk about what you're fixing, what you're cooking with, what he likes to eat and more.

- Ask yourself if the TV is on too much. If so, turn it off and talk!

Talking and having conversations with your child play a necessary part in helping his/her language skills grow.

As Simple as ABC

(For children ages 2 to 6)

Sharing the alphabet with your child helps him begin to recognize the shapes of letters and to link them with the sounds of spoken language. He will soon learn the difference between individual letters — what they look like and what they sound like.

What Parents Need?

- Alphabet books
- ABC magnets
- Paper, pencils, crayons, markers
- Glue and safety scissors

What Can Parents Do?

The first activities in the list below work well with younger children. As your child progresses in age and does the later activities, let him do more. But keep doing the first ones as long as he enjoys them:

- With your toddler sitting with you, print the letters of his name on paper and say each letter as you write it. Make a name sign for his room or other special place. Have him decorate the sign by pasting stickers or drawing on it.
- Teach your child "The Alphabet Song" and play games with him using the alphabet. Some alphabet books have songs and games that you can learn together.

- Look for educational videos, DVDs, CDs, and TV shows such as "Between the Lions" that feature letter-learning activities for young children. Watch such programs with your child and join with him on the rhymes and songs.
- Place alphabet magnets on your refrigerator or on another smooth, safe metal surface. Ask your child to name the letters he plays with and to say the words he may be trying to spell.
- Wherever you are with your child, point out individual letters in signs, billboards, posters, food containers, books, and magazines. When he is 3 to 4 years' old, ask him to begin finding and naming some letters.
- When your child is between ages 3 and 4, encourage him to spell and write his name. For many children, their names are the first words they write. At first, your child may use just one or two letters for his name (for example, Pia, nicknamed Pi, uses the letter *P*).
- Make an alphabet book with your kindergartner. Have him draw pictures (you can help). You can also cut pictures from magazines or use photos. Paste each picture in the book. Help your child to write next to the picture the letter that stands for the object or person in the picture (for example, *B* for bird, *M* for milk, and so on).

When you show your child letters and words over and over again, he will identify and use them more easily when learning to read and write. He will be eager to learn when the letters and words are connected to things that are part of his life.

What Happens Next?

(For children ages 2 to 6)

Books with words or actions that appear over and over help your child to predict or tell what will happen next. These are called "predictable" books. Your child will love to figure out the story in a predictable book!

What Parents Need?

- Predictable books with repeated words, phrases, questions, or rhymes

What Can Parents Do?

The first activities in the list below work well with younger children. As your child progresses in age, the later activities let him do more. But keep doing the first ones as long as he enjoys them:

- Read predictable books to your child. Teach him to hear and say repeating words, such as names for colors, numbers, letters, and animals.

- Pick a story that has repeated phrases, such as this example from *The Three Little Pigs*:
  - **Wolf Voice**: *Little pig, little pig, let me come in.*
  - **Little Pig**: *Not by the hair on my chinny-chin- chin!*
  - **Wolf Voice**: *Then I'll huff and I'll puff and I'll blow your house in!*

  Your child will learn the repeated phrase and have fun joining in with you each time it shows up in the story. Pretty soon, he will join in before you tell him.

- Read books that give hints about what might happen next. Such books have your child lifting flaps, looking through cut-out holes in the pages, "reading" small pictures that stand for words (called "rebuses"), and searching for many other clues. Get excited along with your child as he hurries to find out what happens next.

- When reading predictable books, ask your child what he thinks will happen. See if he points out picture clues, if he mentions specific words or phrases, or if he connects the story to something that happens in real life. These are important skills for a beginning reader to learn.

Help your child develop a sense of responsibility towards books. He should keep a track of the books he has lent from his friends and be mindful about returning the borrowed books on time and that too in the same condition when the books came to his hands.

Predictable books help children to understand how stories progress. A child easily learns familiar phrases and repeats them, pretending to read. Pretend reading gives a child a sense of power and the courage to keep trying.

A Home for My Books

(For children ages 2 to 6)

Starting a home library for your child shows him how important books are. Having books of his own in a special place boosts the chance that your child will want to read even more.

What Parents Need?

- Books from bookstores, garage sales, flea markets, used book stores, and sales at your local library
- A bookcase, a cardboard box, or other materials to make a place for books

What Can Parents do?

Pick a special place for your child's books so that he knows where to look for them. A cardboard box that you can decorate together might make a good book case. Or, you might clear one of the family bookshelves and make a special place for him to put his books.

- Help your child to arrange his books in some order—his favorite books, books about animals, holiday books. Use whatever method will help him find the book easily he looking for.

After returning from a holiday, encourage your child to create a story about holiday. Record it, or get it typed and publish it with Gullybaba.

- It is never easy to find out all the books in the market that are important for your child. Get catalogue of top publishers who publish children books or simply visit gullybaba.com/kids to find book for every occasion.

- Encourage family members and friends to give books to your child as presents for birthdays and other occasions.

  Give books as rewards for performing well in school.

- When you and your child make your own books, you can add them to your home library.

When collecting and reading books are a part of family life, you send your child a message that books are important, enjoyable, and full of new things to learn.

A Picture's Worth a Thousand Words

(For children ages 3 to 6)

Books that have no words, just beautiful pictures, invite you and your child to use your imaginations to make up your own stories to go with the pictures.

What Parents Need?

- Wordless picture books
- Old magazines
- Safety scissors
- Construction paper

What Can Parents Do?

The first activities in the list below work well with younger children. As your child progresses in age and takes interest in later activities, let him do more. But keep doing the first ones as long as he enjoys them:

- Look through the whole picture book with your child. Ask him what he thinks the story is about. Tell the story together by talking about each page as each of you sees it.
- Ask your child to identify objects, animals, or people on each page. Talk with him about the pictures, and ask him if he thinks that they are like real life.

- Have your child tell another child or family member a story using a wordless picture book.

Doing this will make him feel like a "reader" and encourage him to continue learning to read.

- Have your child create his own picture book with his drawings or pictures that you help him cut from magazines.

Using wordless picture books can help improve children's language skills and spark their imaginations.

Rhyme with Me: It's Fun, You'll See!

(For children ages 3 to 6)

Rhyming activities help your child to pay attention to the sounds in words.

What Parents Need?

- Books with rhyming words, word games, or songs

What Can Parents Do?

The first activities in the list below work well with younger children. As your child progresses in age and takes interest in later activities, let him do more. But keep doing the first ones as long as he enjoys them.

Play rhyming games and sing rhyming songs with your child. Many songs and games include clapping, bouncing and tossing balls, and playing in groups.

- Read rhymes to your child. As you read, stop before a rhyming word and encourage your child to fill in the blank. When he does, praise him.
- Listen for rhymes in songs that you know or hear on the radio, TV, or at family or other gatherings. Sing the songs with your child.
- Around the home, point to objects and say their names, for example, *clock*. Then ask your child to say as many words as he can that rhyme with the name. Other easily rhymed words are *ball, bed, rug, sink,* and *toy*. Let your child use some silly, or nonsense, words as well: *toy — joy, boy, woy, loy, doy, hoy, noy.*
- Say three words such as *go, dog,* and *frog,* and ask your child which words sound the same rhyme.
- If your child has an easy-to-rhyme name, ask him to say words that rhyme with it: *Jill — bill, mill, fill, hill.*

- If a computer is available, encourage your child to use it to play rhyming games.

Children around the world have fun with rhyming games and songs. Find lots of books with rhymes and songs.

Match My Sounds

(For children ages 3 to 6)

Listening for and saying sounds in words will help your child to learn that spoken words are made up of sounds, which gets him ready to match spoken sounds to written letters —an important first step towards becoming a reader.

What Parents Need?

- Books with nursery rhymes, tongue twisters, word games, or silly songs

What Can Parents Do?

The first activities in the list below work well with younger children. As your child progresses in age and takes interest in later activities, let him do more. But keep doing the first ones as long as he enjoys them.

- Say your child's name, then have him say words that begin with the same sound; for example: *Daddy— day, doll, dish; Jolly —juice, jam, jar.*
- As you read a story or poem, ask your child to listen for and say the words that begin with the same sound. Then have him think of and say another word that begins with a different sound.

- Read or say a familiar nursery rhyme such as "Humpty, Dumpty." Then have your child make it "Bumpty, Lumpty" or "Thumpty, Gumpty."
- Help your child to make up and say silly lines with lots of words that start with the same sound, such as, "Sister saw six silly snakes."
- Say two names for an animal, and tell your child to choose the name that begins with the same sound as the animal's name. Ask, for example, should a horse's name be Hank or Tank? Should a hen be Mattie or Patty? Should a zebra be Zap or Cap?

Helping children learn to pay attention to sounds in words can prevent reading problems later on.

Attention span of babies is limited. Three minutes of reading is enough for most babies. But, the good thing is that it can be expanded.

Take a Bow!

(For children ages 3 to 6)

When your child acts out a poem or story, he shows his own understanding of what it is about. He also grows as a reader by connecting emotions with written words.

What Parents Need?

- Poems or stories written from a child's point of view
- Things to use in a child's play (dress-up clothes, puppets)

What Can Parents Do?

- Read a poem slowly to your child. Read it with feeling, making the words seem important.
- If your child has a poem he especially likes, ask him to act it out. Ask him to make a face to show the way the character in the poem is feeling. Making different faces adds emotion to the performer's voice. After his performance, praise him for doing a good job.
- Tell your child that the family would love to see his performance of poem. Set a time when everyone can be together. When your child finishes his performance, encourage him to take a bow as everyone claps and cheers loudly.
- Encourage your child to make up his own play from a story that he has read or heard. Tell

him that it can be make-believe or from real life. Help him to find or make things to go with the story — a pretend crown, stuffed animals, a broomstick, or whatever the story needs. Some of his friends or family also can help. You can write down the words or, if he is old enough, help him to write them. Then help him to stage the play for everyone to see!

Play acting helps a child learn that there are more and less important parts to a story. He also learns how one thing in a story

Family Stories

(For children ages 3 to 6)

Telling family stories lets your child know about the people who are important to him. They also give him an idea of how one thing leads to another in a story.

What Can Parents do?

The first activities in the list below work well with younger children. As your child progresses in age, the later activities let him do more. But keep doing the first ones as long as he enjoys them.

- Tell your child stories about your parents and grandparents or about others who are special to you and your family. You might put these stories in a book and add photographs.
- Think out loud about when you were little. Make a story out of something that happened, such as a

family trip, a birthday party, or when you lost your first tooth.

- Have your child tell you stories about what he did on special days, such as holidays, birthdays, and family vacations.
- If you go on a trip, write a trip journal with your child to make a new family story. Take photographs of special events. Writing down special events and pasting photographs of the events in the journal will tie the family story to a written history. You can also include everyday trips, such as going to the grocery store or the park.

The storyteller's voice helps your child to hear the sounds of words and how they are put together to make meaning.

Write On!

(For children ages 3 to 6)

Reading and writing support each other. The more your child does of each, the better he will be at both.

What Parents Need?

- Pencils, crayons, or markers
- Yarn or ribbon
- Writing paper or notebook
- Cardboard or heavy paper
- Construction paper
- Safety scissors

What Can Parents Do?

The first activities in the list below work well with younger children. As your child progresses in age, let him do later activities more. But keep doing the first ones as long as he enjoys them:

- Write with your child. He will learn a lot about writing by watching you write. Talk with him about your writing so that he begins to understand that writing means something and has many uses.
- Have your pre-schooler use his way of writing perhaps just a scribble — to sign birthday cards or make lists.
- Hang a family message board in the kitchen. Offer to write notes there for your child. Be sure that he finds notes left there for him.
- Ask your pre-schooler to tell you simple stories as you write them down. Question him if you don't understand something.

- Encourage your pre-schooler to write his name and practice writing it with him. Remember, at first he may use only the first letter or two of his name.

- Help your child write notes or e-mails to relatives and friends to thank them for gifts or to share his thoughts. Encourage the relatives and friends to answer your child.
- When he is in kindergarten, your child will begin to write words the way he hears them. For example, he might write *haf* for *have*, *frn* for *friend*, and *Frd* for *Friday*. Ask him to read his writing to you. Don't be concerned with correct spelling. He will learn that later.
- As your child progresses in age, he can begin to write or tell you longer stories. Ask questions that will help him to organize the stories. Answer questions about alphabet letters and spelling.
- Turn your child's writing into books. Paste his drawings and writings on pieces of construction paper. For each book, make a cover out of heavier paper or cardboard, then add special art, a title, and his name as author. Punch holes in the pages and cover and bind the book together with yarn or ribbon.

When a child is just beginning, he tries different ways to write and spell. Our job as parents is to encourage our children's writing so they can enjoy putting their thoughts and ideas on paper. Provide them with spelling help when they ask for it.

xxx

4 OTHER WAYS TO HELP

"History will judge us by the difference we make in the everyday lives of children."
~ Nelson Mandela

All of the activities discussed so far offer a rich experience for children as they build their language skills. But you can do even more to support your child's learning.

Make a Bookshelf

This is a must! If you want to make your child a spontaneous reader, the surest way to do it is to give him the authority of some books. Make a bookshelf for your child and fill the books with the picture of babies, animals, surrounding, things of utilities so on and so forth. Even if there is no content in book, the mere images will suffice.

The Librarian

Introduce yourself and your child to your librarian. Librarians can help you to select the best books that are both fun and suitable for your child's age level. They can also show you the other programs and services the library has to offer.

Books . . . and More

In addition to a wealth of books, your library most likely will have tapes and CDs of books, musical CDs and tapes, movies, computers that you can use, and many more resources. You also might find books in languages other than English, or programs to help children improve their reading. If you would like reading help for yourself or your family, check with the librarian about literacy programs in your community.

Take your child to a storytelling session. In the session, the child will enjoy the stories, get analytical abilities and interact with his peer group.

Supervised Story Times

- ***Babies and Toddlers:*** Many libraries have group story hours that are short and geared to the attention spans of the children. During story hour, child sits in your lap, and both of you can join in the story. The storyteller also may show you finger plays and rhythm activities. The storyteller also may give you tips and handouts that you can use for your own home story hours.

- ***Pre-schoolers:*** The library may offer these story hours more than once a week. For these story hours, you and your child usually read several books on the same topic. You might play games, sing songs, use puppets, or do other activities that are connected to that topic. You also may get ideas for books to read and other things to do with your child at home.
- ***Families:*** Families can read together, or they may join in a story told by the library storyteller. Some libraries also set up family activities around the readings, including crafts and art projects and watching movies.

Summer Reading

After the school year is over, some children may forget what they have learned about reading. Libraries help keep children interested in reading by offering summer programs. Children from early elementary school to high school read books on their own. A teacher or librarian may give a child a diary or log in which he may write what he read during the summer. And, because reading aloud is so important to promoting a love of reading, many libraries offer "Read-to-Me" clubs for pre-school and younger children.

Flip through the book you are planning to buy for your child to check its illustrations, language, grammar, etc.

Learning with Computers

Computers can't replace the reading and writing activities discussed earlier in this book. But computers can support what these activities teach your child. Many computer programs (also called software) offer activities that can both grab your child's interest and teach good lessons. Children as young as 3 years' old, though they can't read yet, may still have fun using some of the colorful, action-filled programs with enjoyable characters. Computer reading programs let your child:

- Hear stories, read along and read by himself.
- Play with objects and characters on the screen that teach the alphabet, simple words, rhyming words and other skills important to learning to read.
- Command the computer with his voice, record himself reading and play back the recording so that he can hear himself.

- Write simple sentences and make up stories.
- Add pictures and characters to his stories and have them read back.
- Make and print his own books.
- Make slide shows.
- Gain praise and see improvement in his language abilities.

Finding and Using a Computer

If you do not have a computer at home, you need not lose your heart, for there are plenty of resources available for your help. Firstly, you can find out whether a computer system available in the school library. Most of the schools of today do have a library with computer systems. These computer systems have various software installed and these software are very useful for the kids of today.

If you pay a visit to the school once you will come to know about the library, its timing, computers available there and what is the charge (if any) for operating those computer systems. The school may have computer professionals, adequately knowledgeable and competent to hip your child take optimum help out of the computer. Moreover, if your child uses the computer of his school, he will remain focused on his system, sans any kind of distractions.

Taking Charge of TV

Many children enjoy TV, and they can learn from it. Keep in mind, though, that young children often imitate what they see, good or bad. It's up to you to decide how much TV and what kinds of shows your child should watch.

- Taking into consideration the age of your child, choose the types of things that you want him to see, learn, and imitate.
- Look for TV shows that:
  - teach your child something,
  - hold his interest,
  - encourage him to listen and question,
  - help him learn more words,
  - make him feel good about himself, and
  - introduce him to new ideas and things.

- 'ART ATTACK', 'Chhota bheem' 'Takes his castle" are some shows that you may want to consider. Many other good children's programs are available on public television stations and on cable channels such as the Disney Channel, Cartoon network, HUNAGMA, POGO and Nickelodeon. There are interesting programs on DISCOVERY CHANNEL too.

- Limit the time that you let your child watch TV. Too much television cuts into important activities in a child's life, such as reading, playing with friends, and talking with family members.
- Watch TV with your child when you can. Talk with him about what you see. Answer his questions. Try to point out the things in TV programs that are like your child's everyday life.
- When you can't watch TV with your child, spot check to see what he is watching. Ask questions after the show ends. See what excites him and what troubles him. Find out what he has learned and remembered.
- Try to find books online and offline that explore the themes of the TV shows that your child watches. Or help your child to use his drawings or pictures cut from magazines to make a book based on a TV show.

It is important to help your child develop active reading habits because reading is the cornerstone of all learning.

"The more that you read, the more things you will know. The more you learn, the more places you'll go."

The Benefits or Reading are both Cerebral and Emotional: reading makes you smarter and it keeps you sharp as you age; it boosts analytical skills; increases vocabulary; improves writing skills and memory.

Reading is also a great escape from life's everyday stresses! The love of reading is the single most important gift a parent can give a child.

From the time a baby can sit up, parents can begin to develop active reading habits in their child. Hold them close and read, talk and sing to them. Almost immediately, your baby will start to react to mirrors and pictures of faces, shapes, colors.

By six to twelve months of age, your baby will seek tactile responses and want to touch the book, or place it in his or her mouth. As the child progresses in age, he will enjoy the basic stories contained within the pages of the books. All of these responses are helping to develop active reading habitsin your child.

Most libraries have mom-tot programs that incorporate a thematic story time and book selection to help you develop active reading habits with your child.

Seek out activities at your local library or books' store. They are important first steps in growing the love of reading books.

Unfortunately, when children starts going to school, reading tends to become an arduous task. In our world of instant gratification, we fail to remember that children learn to read step-by-step in a process that takes time and patience; each child grasps the concepts at his or her own pace.

Children who are slow to catch on may feel dejected; they are subjected to reading aloud in class, sent to visit reading specialists and judged by other children unfairly.

It is easy to see why active reading habits may become a dreaded activity, especially when homework includes keeping a daily reading log.

At home reading activities should be casual, creative and stress-free. Leave a newspaper on the counter and mention that you had begun to read an article; ask him or her to read it to you.

Have them spell out any words they are unsure of. While cooking dinner or making a special dessert, let your child read the recipe out-loud.

When shopping, let them read the circulars, food labels, or birthday cards, before selecting the right one. If done right, your child may not even know your ulterior motivation.

The most obvious benefit of active reading habits is that practice makes perfect; the more you read the more accomplished you become.

The following tips will help your child develop active reading habits:

- **Focus on One Sentence at a Time.** For many students, seeing too many words on the page becomes distracting, causing your child to lose his or her place. An index card or blank piece of paper can be used to cover everything except the sentence that your child is reading. When they finish a line, move the card down and repeat the process.

- **Point to the Words.** Encourage your child to follow their reading with their finger, or unsharpened pencil. This technique is beneficial to visual learners. Eventually they will recognize the repetition of a word in context.
- **Take Turns Reading out Loud or Mouth the Words.** When reading at home, you're your child read out load. Whenever possible, switch places and read out load to them. For auditory learners, hearing the words as they are visualized will improve comprehension.
- **Discuss What You Read.** Close the book and ask your child take a few minutes to explain what he or she just read. If the text is pertinent to an exam, help your child by writing a few notes to review. Both techniques will help him or her to retain the information and recall it the next day.
- **Lead by Example**. Shut off the television and read side by side. If your child has a mandated 15 minutes per night, use that time to catch up on your reading. Better yet, go to the library and take out a book. Show your child that reading can be as entertaining as a sitcom.

In the world of video games, Kindles and computers, sitting quietly with a book can appear to a boring activity.

Nurturing the love of reading by developing active reading habits will ensure that your emergent reader understands what he or she is reading and will prepare them for a lifetime of entertainment.

xxx

Having a baby is a life-changer. It gives you a whole other perspective on why you wake up every day.

~Taylor Hanson

5 IF YOU THINK THERE'S A PROBLEM

"The true character of a society is revealed in how it treats its children."
~ Nelson Mandela

Your child may resist being read to or joining with you in the activities in this book. If so, keep trying the activities, but keep them playful. Remember that children vary a great deal in the ways that they learn. Don't be concerned if your child doesn't enjoy a certain activity that his friend of the same age loves. It is important, though, to keep an eye on how your child is progressing.

When a child is having a language or reading problem, the reason might be simple to understand and deal with or it might be complicated and require expert help. Often, children may just need more time to develop their language skills. On the other hand, some children might have trouble seeing, hearing, or speaking. Others may have a learning disability. If you think your child may have some kind of physical or learning problem, it is important to get expert help quickly if your own way does not work.

If your child is in school and you think that he should have stronger language skills, ask for a private meeting with his teacher. In most cases, the teacher or perhaps the principal will be able to help you to understand how your child is doing and what you might do to help him.

(Right to Education does not correlate with the paragraph). Your child might qualify to receive help from a speech and language therapist or other specialist, or he might qualify to receive materials designed to match his needs. You can learn about your special educational rights and responsibilities by requesting that the school gives you — in your first language — a summary of legal rights. To find out about programs for children with disabilities those are available in your state, contact The National Commission for Elementary Education.

The good news is that no matter how long it takes; most children can learn to read. Parents, teachers, and other professionals can work together to determine if a child has a learning disability or other problem, and then provide the right help as soon as possible. When a child gets such help, chances are very good that he will develop the skills he needs to succeed in school and in life. *Nothing is more important than your support for your child as he goes through school. Make sure he gets any extra help he needs as soon as possible and always encourage him and praise his efforts.*

Watching Your Child Progress:

As a parent, you can learn a lot about your child's learning and watch for signs of possible problems. Here are some things to look for and to discuss with his teacher:

- *Starting at age 3 or 4:* Does your child remember nursery rhymes, and can he play rhyming games?
- *At about age 4:* Can your child get information or directions from conversations or books that are read aloud to him?
- *Kindergartners:* Is your child beginning to name and write the letters and numbers that he sees in books, on billboards and signs, and in other places?
- *At age 5:* Can your child play and enjoy simple word games in which two or more words start with the same sound? For example: "Name all the animals you can think of that start with *d*."

At ages 5 and 6: Does your child show that he understands that spoken words can be broken down into smaller parts (for example, by noticing the word *big* in *bigger*)? Does he seem to understand that you can change a small part of a word and make a different word (for example, by changing the first sound and letter of *cat*, you can make *hat, sat, mat, bat, rat,* and so on)?

xxx

6

A READING CHECKLIST

"Children are our second chance to have a great parent-child relationship."
~ *Laura Schlessinger*

There are many ways through which you can encourage your child to become a reader. Here are some questions that you can ask yourself to make sure that you are keeping on track:

For Babies

(6 weeks to 1 year)

- Do I provide a comfortable place for our story time? Is my child happy to be in this place?
- Am I showing my child the pictures in the book? Am I changing the tone of my voice as I read to show emotion and excitement?
- Am I paying attention to how my child responds? What does he especially like? Is he tired and ready to stop?

For Toddlers

(1 to 3 years)

All of the questions above, plus:

- Does my child enjoy the book we are reading?
- Do I encourage my child to "pretend read," joining in where he has memorized a word or phrase?
- When I ask questions, am I giving my child enough time to think and answer?
- Do I tie ideas in the book to things that are familiar to my child? Do I notice if he does this on his own?
- Do I let my child know how much I like his ideas and encourage him to tell me more?
- Do I point out letters, such as the first letter of his name?

For Pre-schoolers

(3 and 4 years)

All of the questions above, plus:

- Do I find ways to help my child begin to identify sounds and letters and to make letter-sound matches?

For Kindergartners

(5 years)

All of the questions above, plus:

- Do I find ways to help my child begin to identify some printed words?
- Do I let my child retell favorite stories to show that he knows how the story develops and what's in it?

For Beginning First-Graders

(6 years)

All of the questions above, plus:

- Do I give my child the chance to read a story to me using the print, picture clues, his memory — or any combination of these ways that help him make sense of the story?

It is important to help your child develop active reading habits because reading is the cornerstone of all learning.

"The more that you read, the more thins you will know. The more you learn, the more places you'll go."

The benefits or reading are both cerebral and emotional: reading makes you smarter and it keeps you sharp as you age; it boosts analytical skills; increases vocabulary; improves writing skills and memory.

Reading is also a great escape from life's everyday stresses! The love of reading is the single most important gift a parent can give a child.

From the time a baby can sit up, parents can begin to develop **active reading habits** in their child. Hold them close and read, talk and sing to them. Almost immediately, your baby will start to react to mirrors and pictures of faces, shapes, colors.

By six to 12 months of age, your baby will seek tactile responses and want to touch the book, or place it in his or her mouth. As the child progresses in age, he or she will enjoy the basic stories contained within the pages of the books. All of these responses are helping to develop *active reading habits* in your child.

Most libraries have mom-tot programs that incorporate a thematic story time and book selection to help you develop active reading habits with your child.

Seek out activities at your local library or books store. They are important first steps in growing the love of reading books.

Unfortunately, when children go to school, reading tends to become an arduous task. In our world of instant gratification, we fail to remember that children learn to read step-by-step in a process that takes time and patience; each child grasps the concepts at his or her own pace.

Children who are slow to catch on may feel dejected; they are subjected to reading aloud in class, sent to visit reading specialists and judged by other children unfairly.

It is easy to see why active reading habits may become a dreaded activity, especially when homework includes keeping a daily reading log.

At home reading activities should be casual, creative and stress-free. Leave a newspaper on the counter and mention that you had begun to read an article; ask him or her to read it to you.

Have them spell out any words they are unsure of. While cooking dinner or making a special dessert, let your child read the recipe out-loud.

When shopping, let them read the circulars, food labels, or birthday cards, before selecting the right one. If done right, your child may not even know your ulterior motivation.

The most obvious benefit of active reading habits is that practice makes perfect; the more you read the more accomplished you become.

The following tips will help your child develop active reading habits:

- **Focus on one sentence at a time:** For many students, seeing too many words on the page becomes distracting, causing your child to lose his or her place. An index card or blank piece of paper can be used to cover everything except the sentence that your child is reading. When they finish a line, move the card down and repeat the process.
- **Point to the words:** Encourage your child to follow their reading with their finger, or unsharpened pencil. This technique is beneficial to visual learners. Eventually they will recognize the repetition of a word in context.
- **Take turns reading out loud or mouth the words:** When reading at home, you're your child read out load. Whenever possible, switch places and read out load to them. For auditory learners, hearing the words as they are visualized will improve comprehension.
- **Discuss what your read:** Close the book and ask your child take a few minutes to explain what he or she just read. If the text is pertinent to an exam, help your child by writing a few notes to review. Both techniques will help him or her to retain the information and recall it the next day.

- **Lead by example:** Shut off the television and read side by side. If your child has a mandated 15 minutes per night, use that time to catch up on your reading. Better yet, go to the library and take out a book. Show your child that reading can be as entertaining as a sitcom.

In the world of video games, Kindles and computers, sitting quietly with a book can appear to a boring activity.

Nurturing the love of reading by developing active reading habits will ensure that your emergent reader understands what he or she is reading and will prepare them for a lifetime of entertainment.

> Remember: Children learn step by step in a process that takes time and patience. They vary a great deal in what holds their interest and in the rate at which they make progress.

> "A nurturing parent protects and teaches their child to survive and thrive in the kind of society in which they will live."

7 TYPICAL LANGUAGE ACCOMPLISHMENTS FOR CHILDREN, BIRTH TO AGE 6

"Parenting is the most important job on the planet next to keeping Gary Busey off the nation's highways."
~ Dennis Miller

Learning to read is built on a foundation of language skills that children start to learn at birth — a process that is both complicated and amazing. Most children develop certain skills as they move through the early stages of learning language. By age 7, most children are reading.

The following list of accomplishments is based on current scientific research in the fields of reading, early childhood education and child development. Studies continue in their fields, and there is still much to learn. As you look over the accomplishments, keep in mind that children vary a great deal in how they develop and learn. If you have questions or concerns about your child's progress, talk with the child's doctor, teacher or a speech and language therapist. For children with any kind of learning problem, the sooner they can get the special help they need, the easier it will be for them to learn.

From birth to age 3, most babies and toddlers become able to:

- Make sounds that imitate the tones and rhythms that adults use when talking.
- Respond to gestures and facial expressions.
- Begin to associate words they hear frequently with what the words mean.
- Make cooing, babbling sounds in the crib, which gives way to enjoying rhyming and nonsense word games with a parent or caregiver.
- Play along in games such as "peek-a-boo" and "pat- a-cake."
- Handle objects such as board books and alphabet blocks in their play.
- Recognize certain books by their covers.

- Pretend to read books.
- Understand how books should be handled.
- Share books with an adult as a routine part of life.
- Name some objects in a book.
- Talk about characters in books.
- Look at pictures in books and realize they are symbols of real things.
- Listen to stories.
- Ask or demand that adults read or write with them.
- Begin to pay attention to specific print such as the first letters of their names.
- Scribble with a purpose (trying to write or draw something).
- Produce some letter-like forms and scribbles that resemble, in some way, writing.

From ages 3-4, most pre-schoolers become able to:

- Enjoy listening to and talking about storybooks.
- Understand that print carries a message.
- Make attempts to read and write.

- Identify familiar signs and labels.
- Participate in rhyming games.
- Identify some letters and make some letter-sound matches.
- Use known letters (or their best attempt to write the letters) to represent written language especially for meaningful words like their names or phrases such as "I love you."

At age 5, most kindergartners become able to:

- Sound as if they are reading when they pretend to read.
- Enjoy being read to.
- Retell simple stories.
- Use descriptive language to explain or to ask questions.
- Recognize letters and letter- sound matches.
- Show familiarity with rhyming and beginning sounds.
- Understand that print is read left-to-right and top-to bottom.

- Begin to match spoken words with written ones.
- Begin to write letters of the alphabet and some words they use and hear often.
- Begin to write stories with some readable parts.

At age 6, most first-graders can:

- Read and retell familiar stories.
- Use a variety of ways to help with reading a story such as rereading, predicting what will happen, asking questions, or using visual cues or pictures.
- Decide on their own to use reading and writing for different purposes.
- Read some things aloud with ease.
- Identify new words by using letter-sound matches, parts of words and their understanding of the rest of a story or printed item.
- Identify an increasing number of words by sight.
- Sound out and represent major sounds in a word when trying to spell.
- Write about topics that mean a lot to them.

- Try to use some punctuation marks and capitalization.

Tips to Introduce Reading to a Differently-abled Child

General rules and guidelines do not work for a differently-abled child. And most alarming thing associated with these children is that they do not get diagnosed early. And this proves to be more painful. A child with hearing disabilities keep on getting rebuked from their teachers, parents for not being able to write properly by hearing the words. Likewise, a child with impaired vision gets reprimand by his teachers, elders, etc. for not being able to write what is written on whiteboard. These types of children keep on getting poor marks year by year and their parents accept that their child is very weak in study.

In fact, the children that fall in this category, needs quick medical attention and sophisticated ways of learning.

Reading to a Visually Impaired Child: In order to make a visually-impaired child read, it is important to use his hearing abilities, instead of his vision. He can be made to write all and well if he is asked to read by listening, and not by seeing.

Reading to a Hard-of Hearing Child: In order to make a hard-of hearing child read, it is imperative to make good use of his eyes. These types of children should be given books and be asked to read by seeing, like reading through the books which is in front of him. There is nothing to be worried about these children. The only thing that is a no-no in this case is to dictate him to write.

In addition to these, take the feelings of your child seriously. Try not to tell, “Reading is not Cup of your Tea”.

Some Basic Tips that can be Followed and Practised

1. **Parents should Read with Children:** Everything a child learns starts at home, with the family. Unless and until there is some parental involvement, children are not going to develop any habits. When it comes to inculcating reading habits in children, the first thing that parents would have to do is to enforce it upon them. They should make it a point to sit down and read with the children. At an early age, **parents should try reading out to the children** in order to get their children reading on their own. This practice at an early age, can build comprehension of words, increase their vocabulary and make the children more confident about picking up a book themselves.

2. **Make Reading Material Easily Available:** If you want to make your children read more, you have to make sure that they have something to read. Chances are higher that children who are surrounded by books would be more inclined to

pick them up and read them. Of course, the books that you surround the children with should be related to their age as well. Make sure that the **books that you have gotten for your children would be attractive and appealing** to them and not something too tough for their reading level. Put some books in the living room, family room, the child's bedroom .

3. **Have Reading Activities Planned:** Children usually do not read because they don't think it is fun or cool. So, as a parent or a teacher, you can come up with some **activities to get the children reading**. You could have some interactive reading sessions planned out, or you could make the children draw what they have read once they have read it. You can pretty much do any activity to get your children reading, as long as you are sure that your child would like it.

4. **Start Small:** You can't really make them start reading books right from the bat, which means that the watch word should now be starting small and easy. Kids will not be interested to develop a reading habit if they are intimidated by it, so start off with something small.

   When you are watching TV, make them read out the various things that come on the screen. When you are at a restaurant, make them read the menu and tell you what they want. Small things like these might not make your children become engrossed in books within days, but slowly, it will make them more confident. And **confidence is what wins the day when the reading habit of children is to be cultivated**.

5. **Take your Children to the Bookstore:** You know how children always have an inclination to want something that they are surrounded by? You walk past a toy store; they will certainly demand something that is on the shelf. You can apply the same tactic for books as well. If you expose your children to bookstores and libraries, they will certainly be inclined to take a look at them and even develop an interest in them! They will even start asking for new reading material soon enough and boom, you have learnt **how to make children read.**

6. **Take Your Child to the Library:** The library is a wonderful place to cultivate reading habits in children. There are so many books there that some are bound to catch your child's attention. Most libraries have free membership and even if you have to pay, it is barely legible fee! This way, you can **get your child into the habit of reading** and loving it, without really spending too much.

7. **Acknowledge the Child's Progress and Success:** Praise and prizes can go a long way in cultivating a habit. So, when you

are **encouraging reading habits in children**, you should also appreciate it when they do complete reading a book. Reward them something they really like and they will certainly be motivated to read more. As they grow up, they will stop needing this extra motivation or the extra prize, because by now, they will already be used to reading so much.

8. **As a Teacher, Assign Reading Problems:** One of the biggest causes that contribute towards the lack of reading awareness among children is the fact that when they are in school, they are never really involved in any reading activities. Reading activities are related to studies as well and one of the **best ways to encourage children to develop a reading habit** is to make sure that they would be awarded academically by the same.

9. **Make use of Technology:** There was a point of time when you would have had to use only books to encourage children to read. Most books were not really aimed at children as well, which would prove to be quite a headache for parents and teachers who were trying to make children read. However, there are plenty many options for parents now. Reading can be encouraged, not only through books but also through visual aids, audio books, book DVDs etc. **Using media and technology the right way could definitely help develop a reading habit.**

10. **Make Reading an Example:** Children always learn from what the adults around them are doing. So, if you want to know how to make children read, you should keep in mind that you do the same. **Unless and until you read, your children might not be that motivated to read themselves**. We know that you might not have done the same when you were a child, but all you have to do is pick up a book and sit with your child when they are reading. You could either spend some quality time with your child, reading the same thing that you are reading too. Or you could just give your child the books they want to read and read something that you want to read.

Children spend a lot of time at home and they also spend a lot of time at school as well. They have to develop habits in both these places so that they can have a more well- rounded development of the habit. While parents can help in initiating the habit among children, it is teachers who can hone it. After a point of time, the **children must be taught how to apply their reading habits**. They need to know how to apply the things that they learn from reading and they also need to learn how to interpret the world around them in the same terms.

It is essential to develop a reading habit because it provides children with a huge advantage and a benefit. They will not just be able to read, they will have an advantage over most other children when it comes to IQ tests or competitive exams and they will certainly be better world citizens.

One should also keep in mind that it is necessary for parents to realize that each child is different and the amount they can read and the kind of books they can read will vary.

"Love your children more than your ego. Love your children enough to allow them to progress through childhood as non-perfect beings, who are a work in progress, just like you are."

-Nicholeen Peck

RESOURCES FOR FAMILIES AND CAREGIVERS

"My children are the reason I laugh, smile and want to get up every morning."
~ *Gena Lee Nolin*

- **Ministry of Human Resource Development (MHRD)**

  Department of School Education and Literacy

  Shastri Bhawan, New Delhi-110001

  Tel: 91-11-23382587

  Fax 91-11-23387859

  E-mail : webmaster.edu@nic.in

- **Ministry of Women and Child Development**

  6th Floor A Wing, Shastri Bhawan

  New Delhi, 110001

  91-11-23714938/23710140/23387683

- **Ministry of Health and Family Welfare**

  Room No. 348; 'A' Wing, Nirman Bhavan,

  New Delhi-110011

  Tel: 011-23063024, 011-23063513,

  011-23061661

  Fax: 011-23062358

  Email: hfwminister@gov.in (For Letters on Policies, Issues, Suggestions and Grievances) appointments-hfm@gov.in(For seeking Appointments with HFM)

Private Organizations that Deal with Literacy and Reading

- Ekal Vidyalaya Foundation of India

  8, Local Shopping Complex,

  Okhla Industrial Area, Phase -2

  New Delhi - 110020

  Tel: 011 - 40503331

  Email: evfi.office@ekal.org

- **Pratham**

  Pratham Mumbai Education Initiative

  Y B Chavan Centre, 4th Floor,

  General J Bhosale Marg, Nariman Point,

  Mumbai - 400021, Opp. Mantralaya (Map)

NGOS

NGOS For Children

Children Welfare Organisations

Institutions For Educational Assistance

Institutions For Slum Children Education

Tel: 022- 22819562, 22819561

Fax: 022- 22819563

Pratham Resource Center

B-4/58, Safdarjung Enclave, 2nd Floor,

New Delhi-110 029

Tel: 011-26716083/41651638

Resources If Your Child has a Reading Problem or Learning Disability

- **International Reading Association:** www. reading. org
- **The Association of Learning Disabilities of India**

  Reg No. (297/95)

  ALDI Learning Centre

  Nellankara, Nettissery P.O. Thrissur - 680657, India

  Tel: + 91 487 2336817

  E-mail: joseph.aldindia@gmail.com

- **Delhi Learning Disabilities Association**

  Registered Addresses and Administration HQ:

  Orkids Foundation

  E-123, Kalkaji, New Delhi-110019

  Orkids Education Systems Pvt. Ltd.

  A-3, Chirag Enclave, New Delhi-110048

  Orkids Administration HQ

  E-66, Suncity

  Sector 54, Gurugram, Haryana 122001

  Tel: 0124 4006232, 4087937

Resources for the Blind and Physically Handicapped

- **Aashray Adhikar Abhiyan**

  S-442, II Floor, School Block

  Shakarpur, New Delhi-110092

  Fax: (+91)-011-22484618

  Tel: (+91)-011-22483240/1609/1887

  9810711644/9312668807

  Email: creatinghomes@yahoo.co.uk (main office)

  paramkaur8115@gmail.com (Paramjeet)

  sanjaykrishna.sk@gmail.com (Sanjay)

  Website: www.homelesspeople.in

- **Asha Awwa School for Handicapped Children**

  AWWA Secretariat 210, South Block Integrated HQ of Defence (Army) DHQ

  New Delhi, Delhi

  Tel: 011-23018183/23012897

  Email: centralawwa@gmail.com

- **Association for the Development of Multiple Handicapped Children**

  B-56, Defence Colony, New Delhi-110024

  Tel: 462 3548

  Working in the area of Multiple disabilities, cerebral palsy, post polio residual paralysis, intellectual impairment. It has a nursery school and an infant intervention programme. Psychotherapy, physiotherapy and counselling facilities are provided. Vocational training in the areas of computer, clay modelling, drawing, painting, music and drama, is given.

- Child Guidance Center

- Department of Social Work (Delhi Univ.), 3 University Road, New Delhi-1 10009;

  Phone: 2725 7881;

  Focus Area: Multiple disability; Mentally ill; Behavioural problems; Learning disability.

- National Institute of Public Co-Operation & Child Development 5, Siri Institutional Area, Hauz Khas, New Delhi-110016;

  Phone: 2696 3002/3204/3378;

  Focus Area: Multiple disability; Speech problem; Slow learners in the age groups 0-14; Scholastic problems.

- Zakir Hussain Memorial Welfare Society,

  Jamia Millia Islamia (TTT), New Delhi-110025;

  Phone: 26842554(R), 26843909;

  Focus Area: Mentally ill; Behavioural and speech problems; Educational problems.

- RAK College of Nursing, Lajpat Nagar, New Delhi-110024;

  Phone: 2643 6668;

  Focus Area: Mental disability; Psychological problems; Communication disorders.

- Dr. Z.H. Memorial Welfare Soc.,

  Jamia Sr. Sec. School Camps, Jamia Nagar, New Delhi-25;

  Phone: 26843909;

  Focus Area: Multiple disability.

- Kalawati Saran Children's Hospital

  Bangla Sahib Marg, New Delhi-110025;

  Phone: 23735090;

  Focus Area: Multipie disability; Mentally ill; Physical and emotional problems.

- Department of Psychiatry AIIMS

  New Delhi-110029;

  Phone: 26594412;

  Focus Area: Mentally ill; Slow learners; Psychological disorders.

- **Delhi Society for the Welfare of Mentally Retarded Children**

  Okhla Centre, Okhla Marg, opposite Holy Family Hospital, New Delhi-1 10025;

  Phone: 26310979;

  Focus Area: Mentally ill.

- **Handicapped Women's Welfare Association**

  BB 5A, DDA Flats, Shalimar Bagh, New Delhi;

  Phone: 27263218, 27263451;

  Focus Area: Multiple disability in women and children in the age groups 3-40 Years; Hearing impaired; Mentally ill; Orthopaedically handicapped.

- **Hope Foundation**

  D-32, First floor, Jangpura Extension, New Delhi-110014;

  Phone: 24317359, 24314130, 24313047;

  E-mail: ravisharma@hopeww.org; Website: www.HOPEWW.org

  Focus Area: Leprosy; Women and child.

- **Model School for Mentally Deficient Children**

  Kasturba Niketan, Lajpat Nagar, New Delhi-110024;

  Phone: 26834328

  Fax: 26831012;

  Focus Area: Mentally retarded.

- **Muskaan - Parents Assoc. for the Welfare of Children with Mental Handicap**

  Bandra Centre (Administrative Office)

  15 Prashanti, Opposite MHADA Building,

  Near Matoshree Bungalow, Kalanagar,

  Bandra (East), Mumbai 400051.

  Tel: (022) 26592745, +91 9930386115, +91 9930181069

  Goregaon Centre

  Tenement No 20/77, Ground Floor,

Goregaon Yeshwant Nagar Co-operative

Housing Society Ltd.,

Yeshwant Nagar, Off S. V. Road,

Goregaon (West),

Mumbai 400062.

Tel: +91 7506094898

Wadia Centre, Parel

2nd Floor, Baijerbai Wadia Hospital for Children,

Acharya Donde Marg, Lower Parel,

Mumbai 400012.

Tel: +91 88798359

Tel: 022-26592745/9930386115/7506094898

Email: contact@muskanfoundation.org.in

Facebook: facebook.com/muskanfoundation.org

Twitter: twitter.com/muskanngo

Instagram: https://www.instagram.com/muskanfoundatio

Books for Parents

The following books are just a few of the many excellent books on reading with children. Check with your librarian for titles of more books and for children's book lists.

- Beaty, Janice J. Building Bridges with Multicultural Picture Books: For Children 3-5. Prentice-Hall, 1996. Contains a listing of selected multicultural picture books for young children. Includes activities to do with children that are based on the books listed.

- Butler, Dorothy. Babies Need Books: Sharing the Joy of Books with Children from Birth to Six. Heinemann, 1998. Discusses the importance of reading to young children and gives summaries of books by age level.
- Hall, Susan L., and Moats, Louisa C. Straight Talk about Reading: How Parents Can Make a Difference During the Early Years. NTC Publishing Group. 1998. Provides practical advice, games and activities, and lists of children's books and resources that parents can use to help their children read.
- Muse, Daphne (Ed.). The New Press Guide to Multicultural Resources for Young Readers. The New Press, 1997. Includes reviews of hundreds of children's books from a wide variety of backgrounds.
- Trelease, Jim. The Read-Aloud Handbook. Penguin, 2001. Discusses the importance of reading aloud to children. Includes a "Treasury of Read-Alouds"—hundreds of recommended books annotated by age and grade level.

Some Other Informative Websites for Parents and Caregivers

- Family Education Network:

  http://www.familyeducation.com

xxx

RESOURCES FOR CHILDREN

"What can you do to promote world peace?
Go home and love your family."
~ *Mother Teresa*

Here's a sampling of books, computer programs, and Web sites that you and your child can enjoy together. Check with your local librarian for more suggestions.

Babies

- Brown, Margaret Wise. Goodnight Moon. Harper Collins, 1997. A little rabbit says goodnight to all the things in his room and, finally, to the Moon.
- Johnson, Angela. Mama Bird, Baby Birds. Orchard, 1994. Joshua and his sister, two young African–American children, watch a mother bird feeding its babies.

- Wells, Rosemary. Max's Bedtime. Dial, 1998. Even though Max's sister offers him her stuffed animals, he cannot sleep without his red rubber elephant.

Play Books for Toddlers and Preschoolers

- Carle, Eric. The Very Busy Spider. Philomel, 1984. Farm animals try to keep a spider from spinning her web, but she doesn't give up and she makes a beautiful and useful creation. Pictures may be felt as well as seen, making this a great book for visually impaired children.
- Hill, Eric. Where's Spot? Putnam, 1980. In an interactive lift-the-flap book, children help Spot's mother, Sally, search the house to find him. This book has been translated into a number of languages, including a sign language version.
- Kunhardt, Dorothy. Pat the Bunny. Golden Books, 1990. In this touch-and-feel book, Paul and Judy smell the flowers, feel Daddy's scratchy face, look in the mirror, play peek-a-boo, and, of course, pat the bunny.
- Lacome, Julie. Seashore. Candlewick, 1995. Small fingers can poke through the holes in the pages of this board book about the beach, and seem to change into fins, wings, or crawling legs.

Alphabet Books for Pre-schoolers-First-Graders

- Kitamura, Satoshi. From Acorn to Zoo and Everything in Between in Alphabetical Order.

Sunburst, 1995. Each page shows an assortment of things that begin with the same letter—all clearly labeled. For each page there is a question (and a clue) that can be answered only by looking carefully at the picture.

- MacDonald, Suse. Alphabatics. Bradbury Press, 1986. The letters of the alphabet are transformed and placed in 26 illustrations so that the hole in b becomes a balloon and y turns into the head of a yak (an ox with long hair).
- Rankin, Laura. The Handmade Alphabet. Puffin, 1996. This book presents the handshape for each letter of the manual alphabet (American Sign Language) accompanied by an object whose name begins with that letter.
- Shannon, George. Tomorrow's Alphabet. Mulberry Books, 1999. A is for seed—what's going on here? The seed is tomorrow's Apple! An imaginative alphabet puzzle that encourages children to think and make predictions.
- Shelby, Anne. Potluck. Orchard, 1991. A multicultural collection of friends having names starting with A–Z bring a variety of dishes to a potluck.

Wordless Picture Books for Pre-schoolers-First-Graders

- Carle, Eric. Do You Want to Be My Friend? HarperCollins, 1995. A little mouse asks all kinds of animals, "Do you want to be my friend?"

- dePaola, Tomie. Pancakes for Breakfast. Voyager Books, 1990. A little old lady's attempts to have pancakes for breakfast are hindered by a lack of ingredients and the help of her pets.
- Mayer, Mercer. A Boy, a Dog, and a Frog. Econo-Clad Books, 1999. A boy and a dog try unsuccessfully to catch a frog.
- McCully, Emily. School. HarperTrophy, 1990. The eight oldest mice in a family prepare for the first day of school. After everyone leaves, and the house is too quiet, the youngest mouse decides to go discover what school is all about.
- Wiesner, David. Tuesday. Clarion, 1991. One night a town is invaded by extraterrestrial frogs flying in on their lily pads.

Rhyming Books for Toddlers-Kindergartners

- Christelow, Eileen. Five Little Monkeys Jumping on the Bed. Clarion, 1989. This counting rhyme shows five little monkeys getting ready for bed and getting sidetracked by some serious bed-jumping.
- Cole, Joanna, and Calmenson, Stephanie. Eentsy, Weensty Spider: Fingerplays and Action Rhymes. Morrow, 1991. This book, illustrated using children of diverse cultural backgrounds, includes fingerplays and action rhymes that have been chanted, sung, and loved by generations.

- Dyer, Jane. Animal Crackers: A Delectable Collection of Pictures, Poems and Lullabies for the Very Young. Little, Brown, 1996. This picture book contains a collection of Mother Goose classics, modern poems, lullabies, and simple stories, many of which celebrate special times in a child's first years.
- Martin, Bill, Jr., and Archambault, John. Chicka Chicka Boom Boom. Simon & Schuster, 1989. The rhythmical story of letters of the alphabet climbing and falling from a coconut tree.

"Predictable" Books for Toddlers-First-Graders

- Aardema, Verna. Bringing the Rain to Kapiti Plain. Dutton, 1993. Told in verse, this is the story of how Ki-pat, a herder, makes it rain on the dry Kapiti Plain.
- Hutchins, Pat. Rosie's Walk. Macmillan, 1968. Rosie the hen goes for a walk and manages to avoid many attempts on her life by a predatory fox. Also available in Spanish.
- Lowell, Susan. The Three Little Javelinas. Northland Pub., 1993. This southwestern tale, based on "The Three Little Pigs" and illustrated with Native American and Latino characters, is about three little javelinas as they try to outsmart the coyote who had hoped to eat them with red chili sauce.

- Martin, Bill, Jr. Brown Bear, Brown Bear What Do You See? Holt, 1996. What children see is a surprising cast of animals!
- McNaughton, Colin. Suddenly! Harcourt Brace, 1995. Time after time, Preston the Pig outwits a hungry wolf that is trying to catch and eat him.

Multiple-Language Books for Pre-schoolers-First-Graders

- Brown, Ruth. Alphabet Times Four: An International ABC. Dutton, 1991. Beginning with the letter A and ending with Z, this book offers a word that happens to begin with the same letter in four languages, English, Spanish, French, and German, accompanied by creatively bordered pictures.
- Garza, Carmen Lomas. Family Pictures. Children's Book Press, 1990. In this bilingual text (Spanish and English), a young girl remembers her day-to-day family life while growing up in Texas in a Mexican–American culture.
- Hirschi, Ron. Seya's Song. Sasquatch Books, 1992. A young S'Klallam girl follows the seasons of the salmon, interweaving aspects of the life and culture of her Pacific Coast tribe and using words from her native language.
- Lee, Huy Voun. In the Park. Henry Holt & Co, Inc., 1998. Xiao Ming and his mother go to the park, where they see a variety of people of

different cultures, ages, and disabilities. At the park, his mother teaches him how to draw and pronounce some Chinese characters.

- Rattigan, Jama Kim. Dumpling Soup. Little, Brown, 1993. Marisa, a 7-year-old girl who lives in Hawaii, explains the traditions her family celebrates at the New Year. Hawaiian, Japanese, and Korean words and phrases add to the English text.
- Stock, Catherine. Where Are You Going Manyoni? Morrow, 1993. Manyoni lives in Zimbabwe and on her way to school she passes many beautiful areas, wild animals, and birds. The book includes a picture glossary of wildlife and a key to pronouncing African words.

Beginning Readers

- Eastman, P. D. Go, Dog. Go! Random House, 1989. Big dogs, little dogs—black, white, yellow, and blue dogs—they are all very busy going places and doing things.
- Krauss, Ruth. The Carrot Seed. Harper Collins, 1973. A little boy knows a carrot will grow from the seed that he planted no matter what anyone else may say or think.

Early Read-Aloud Chapter Books for Pre-schoolers-First-Graders

- Cameron, Ann. The Stories Julian Tells. Knopf, 1981. Julian tells great stories, He can make people, especially his younger brother Huey, believe almost anything, which sometimes leads to lots of trouble.

- Milne, A. A. The House at Pooh Corner. Dutton, 1991. The book is about the timeless adventures of Pooh, Piglet, Christopher Robin, Owl, Tigger, and Eeyore in the Hundred- Acre Woods.

Children's Magazines

- Babybug: http://www.babybugmag.com
- Click!: http://www.clickmag.com
- Sesame Street Magazin: http://www.ctw.org/sesame/ or http://www2.cdsfulfillment.com/SST/subscriptions.cgi
- Your Big Back Yard: http://www.nwf.org/ybby/

Computer Programs

Living Books: Interactive Animated Stories (Ages 3-7)

These programs provide a place for children to hear a story, read along with the narrator, or read by them. They also can interact with characters and objects and play games that teach the alphabet, simple words, rhyming, and other reading skills. Each program also comes with the matching book. Some examples of titles:

- Just Grandma and Me
- The Cat and the Hat

- Arthur's Birthday
- Dr. Seuss's ABC

Bailey's Book House (Ages 2-5)

This software features Bailey and his friends as they encourage young children to build literacy skills and develop a love for reading. It includes activities to help youngsters explore letters, words, sentences, rhyming, and stories. No reading skills are required; all directions are spoken.

Let's Go Read! An Island Adventure (Ages 4-7)

Children join Robby Raccoon and his friends in their adventures on an island inhabited by the alphabet. Included are activities to help children learn reading basics such as letter sounds and how to sound out and build simple words. Children can command the computer with their voices and record and listen to themselves reading.

Young Children and the Internet: Places to Learn and Play

- Arthur: http://www.pbs.org/wgbh/pages/arthur/
- Disney: http://disney.go.com/park/bases/familybase/today/
- Dr. Seuss's Seussville:

  http://www.randomhouse.com/seussville/university/

- PBS Homepage: http://www.pbs.org/kids/
- Central Zoo Authority: http://www.cza.nic.in/

Understand Your Child: Teen and Child Personality Test

- http://www.personalitylab.org/tests/bfi2_parent_outs.htm

xxx